THE

POCKET

BOOK

A SMALL BOOK OF POWERFUL POSTS

JAMELIAH GOODEN

ISBN: 978-1-960146-07-6

Gooden. Jameliah

Edited by: Amy Ashby

Published by Warren Publishing
Charlotte, NC
www.warrenpublishing.net
Printed in the United States

To my Car Chronicles *followers on Facebook,
all 500,000 of you (and counting!) inspire me
each day,and I would love to dedicate this book
of social media prompts to you. You are just
as much part of my life as I am to yours.
Thank you for allowing me to be your morning
devotion and for allowing me into your lives.*

INTRODUCTION

The pocketbook is a very powerful accessory. If you forget it, you feel lost without it. Designer or not, crossover or clutch, everything you need for your day-to-day life is contained in that one little—or sometimes, not so little—bag. If you leave the house without your pocketbook, you always go back and get it. It's that important.

And so is this little book.

This book's purpose is to provide you with prompts and pick-me-ups you can use for your own self-discovery and journaling—and when you post on social media. Each prompt is followed by blank pages where you can reflect, react, and explore your thoughts. Then, if you'd like, you can share them with others.

If you're like me, you share a lot of your life on social media. We live in a social media society; it's how we stay connected to our family and friends, it's how we meet new people, and it's how we share our thoughts and opinions with others. Social media enables us to feel empowered and to feel heard. So, once you have reflected upon a *Pocketbook* prompt, you can post it so you, your friends, and your followers can discuss and explore together.

It's my hope this small book will create big things. So read, discover, and post with power.

"IF THE GOVERNMENT DOES NOT BELIEVE IN GOD, WHY DO THEY ASK US TO PRAY TO HIM WHEN THEY ARE THE ONES GETTING US IN TROUBLE?"

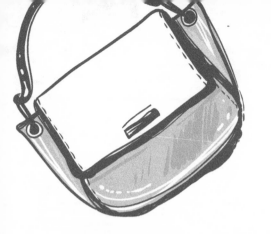

"ACCEPT THE HARD
TRUTHS BEFORE YOU
RECEIVE THE SOFT LIES."

"SOME HEARTBREAKS ARE FROM HEAVEN; GOD MIGHT BREAK YOUR HEART TO SAVE YOUR LIFE."

"HOW DO YOU UNTIE A SOUL
IF YOUR FLESH KEEPS
TIGHTENING THE KNOT?
LOOSEN IT AND LET IT GO."

"DON'T JUST DIVORCE THE PERSON;
DIVORCE YOUR OLD IDENTITY."

"PROCRASTINATION'S BEST FRIEND
IS LAZINESS, AND I WOULD
NOT WANT TO COME TO THEIR PARTY."

"IN ORDER FOR SOMEONE FROM
YOUR PAST TO ENTER YOUR FUTURE,
THEY HAVE TO BE INVITED IN."

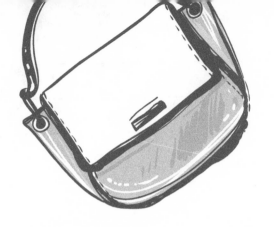

"THE ONLY CLAP BACK A HATER NEEDS TO HEAR IS THE SOUND OF OTHER PEOPLE'S APPLAUSE."

"A JEALOUS PERSON IS THREATED OF WHO YOU'RE BECOMING."

"IT'S HARD TO HEAR GOD
WHEN NEGATIVITY IS
ALWAYS IN YOUR EARS."

"YOU CAN'T SEE A BEAUTIFUL FACE WHEN AN UGLY CHARACTER OVERRIDES IT."

"'BEAUTY IS SKIN DEEP.' MAYBE THAT'S WHY YOU KNOW SO MANY BEAUTIFUL MONSTERS."

"I MIGHT FALL, BUT I WON'T FAIL."

"GOD SEES ME WHEN YOU DON'T. THAT'S WHY, EVEN THOUGH YOU REJECT ME NOW, YOU WILL RESPECT ME LATER."

"A BROKEN HEART CAN HEAL
IN A WEEK; A SHATTERED ONE
TAKES A LIFETIME."

"BEFORE I CAN BE A BETTER HALF,
I HAVE TO BECOME WHOLE.
THERAPY CAN HELP ME GET THERE."

"SACRIFICE IS ABOUT
SAVING US; SELFISHNESS
IS ABOUT SAVING *YOU*."

"THE ONLY MAN WHO CAN
USE ME IS JESUS."

"THE ONLY WOMAN WHO SHOULD TREAT A MAN BETTER THAN HIS MOTHER DOES IS SUPPOSED TO BE HIS WIFE."

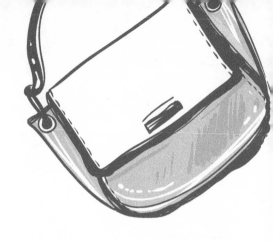

"I REFUSE TO LET LIFE'S PAIN PUSH ME AWAY FROM LIFE'S PLEASURES."

_____

_____

_____

_____

_____

_____

_____

_____

_____

_____

_____

_____

_____

"IF THE FIRST MAN WHO EVER FAILED YOU WAS YOUR FATHER, DON'T LET SOMEONE ELSE'S DAD DO IT TOO."

"LOVE IS EASILY IDENTIFIED
WHEN YOU RECOGNIZE IT
IN YOURSELF FIRST."

"I LOVE MYSELF ENOUGH
TO FORGIVE THE TIMES
I CAUSED MYSELF PAIN."

"I DON'T HAVE TIME TO WASTE ON
THINGS THAT DON'T MATTER; MY
TIME IS FOR THE THINGS THAT DO."

"IF YOU'RE HOLDING YOUR BREATH
WAITING FOR ME TO FAIL, EMAIL
SOMEONE YOUR OBITUARY."

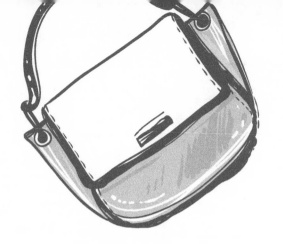

"I MIGHT NOT BE ABLE TO
SAVE THE WORLD,
BUT I CAN SAVE MY OWN."

"I CAN'T SEE THROUGH WALLS AND LIES; TELL THE TRUTH IF YOU WANT ME TO NOTICE YOU."

"REAL LOVE IS EFFORTLESS.
IF IT'S TOO HARD,
IT PROBABLY WON'T WORK."

"I WON'T GIVE UP ON LOVE ... *IF WE HAVE AN UNDERSTANDING ABOUT WHAT WE ARE TRYING TO BUILD.*"

"ANYTHING YOU TRY TO
FORCE WILL EVENTUALLY BREAK."

"PEOPLE WILL ALWAYS HAVE A PROBLEM WITH YOU FALLING IN LOVE ESPECIALLY IF YOU WERE THE PERSON RESPONSIBLE FOR BREAKING THEIR HEART IN THE FIRST PLACE. PAIN WANTS YOU TO ONLY EXPERIENCE PAIN."

"PEOPLE WILL ALWAYS HAVE A PROBLEM WITH A PERSON LOVING SOMEONE THEY CAN SEE. LET ME LOVE *GOD* WHILE YOU AVOID BEING CATFISHES."

"LOVE KEEPS NO RECORD OF WRONG; IF YOU DON'T FORGIVE AND LET IT GO, YOU CAN NEVER MOVE ON."

"IF A PERSON IS NOT HAPPY, THEY
WILL NEVER FEEL FULFILLED BY
THE PERSON THEY LOVE."

"IF YOU DON'T SAVE FOR THE RAINY DAYS, A STORM MIGHT COME BY THAT YOU'RE NOT PREPARED FOR."

"THE GRASS IS ALWAYS GREENER ON THE OTHER SIDE—ESPECIALLY WHEN YOU STOP TAKING CARE OF YOURS."

"THE GOVERNMENT MAY TAKE PRAYER OUT OF THE SCHOOLS BUT IT CAN NEVER TAKE PRAYER OUT OF YOUR HEART."

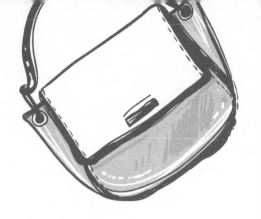

"THE ONLY WAY TO DROWN
OUT A NEGATIVE VOICE IS TO
POUR IN A POSITIVE ONE.
LET FAITH BE IN YOUR
VOCAL CHORDS."

"THE ONLY THING THAT IS IN MY PAST IS MY CHILDHOOD, AND EVEN SOME OF THOSE CHILDHOOD MEMORIES NEED TO BE FORGOTTEN."

"IF IT DOESN'T BENEFIT MY FUTURE,
I WILL LEAVE IT IN THE PAST."

"POSITIVE VIBES WILL NEVER
COME FROM A NEGATIVE PERSON."

"SOME OF LIFE'S GREATEST
BLESSINGS COME
AFTER A BREAKUP."

"YOU WILL NEVER WALK ALONE
AS LONG AS YOU HAVE TWO THINGS:
GOD AND A GOOD PET."

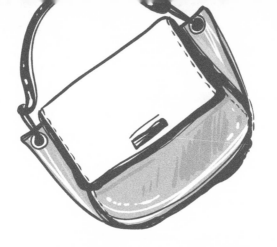

"BE CAREFUL OF THE WORDS YOU SPEAK AND MAKE SURE THEY'RE SWEET; THEY WILL EVENTUALLY FALL BACK ON YOUR PLATE, AND YOU MAY BE FORCED TO EAT THEM."

_____

_____

_____

_____

_____

_____

_____

_____

_____

_____

_____

_____

_____

"IF SOMEONE BROKE YOUR HEART, SIT BACK, RELAX, AND WAIT FOR SOMEONE TO BREAK THEIRS. THE LAW OF RECIPROCITY IS VERY REAL."

"FILL A CUP WITH
POSITIVITY SO THE GOODNESS
OF LIFE CAN POUR OUT."

"PARENTING IS THE HARDEST
JOB YOU CAN SIGN UP FOR.
NO SICK DAYS, NO DAYS OFF,
AND DISGRUNTLED EMPLOYEES
YOU CAN NEVER FIRE."

"FIGHT BACK WHEN SOMEONE
REFUSES TO ACKNOWLEDGE
YOUR STRENGTH."

"THE HARDEST LESSON YOU WILL LEARN THROUGH PARENTING IS TO LET YOUR CHILDREN FALL AND KNOW THAT GOD WON'T LET THEM FAIL."

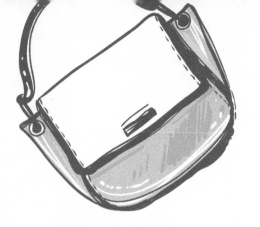

"IF YOU HAD GREAT PARENTS, YOU ARE BLESSED. IF YOU DID NOT, SHOW THEM, BY EXAMPLE, HOW TO BE THE PARENTS THEY SHOULD HAVE BEEN."

"LOVE THE HELL OUT
OF SOMEONE, BY SHOWING
THEM THE HEAVEN IN YOU."

"A CRAZY PERSON WILL FIND OTHER CRAZY PEOPLE TO JUSTIFY THEIR CRAZY, AND WHEN THEY ALL GET TOGETHER, THEY'LL BE A GROUP OF MIXED NUTS."

"IF THE HEART CONTAINS ALL THE COLORS OF THE RAINBOW AND OUR EYES ONLY SEE BLACK AND WHITE. THE WORLD'S PROBLEMS UNFORTUNATELY, ARE SKIN DEEP."